UNDERSTANDING THE PARANORMAL

INVESTIGATING ATLANTIS

AND OTHER LOST CITIES

PHILIP WOLNY

Britannica
Educational Publishing

IN ASSOCIATION WITH

ROSEN
EDUCATIONAL SERVICES

Published in 2015 by Britannica Educational Publishing (a trademark of Encyclopædia Britannica, Inc.) in association with The Rosen Publishing Group, Inc. 29 East 21st Street, New York, NY 10010

Distributed exclusively by Rosen Publishing.
To see additional Britannica Educational Publishing titles, go to rosenpublishing.com.

First Edition

Britannica Educational Publishing
J. E. Luebering: Director, Core Reference Group
Anthony L. Green: Editor, Compton's by Britannica

Rosen Publishing
Hope Lourie Killcoyne: Executive Editor
Jacob R. Steinberg: Editor
Nelson Sá: Art Director
Nicole Russo: Designer
Cindy Reiman: Photography Manager

Cataloging-in-Publication Data

Wolny, Philip.
Investigating Atlantis and other lost cities/Philip Wolny.
    pages cm.—(Understanding the paranormal)
Includes bibliographical references and index.
ISBN 978-1-62275-857-9 (library bound)—ISBN 978-1-62275-858-6 (pbk.)—
ISBN 978-1-62275-860-9 (6-pack)
1. Atlantis (Legendary place)—Juvenile literature. 2. Extinct cities—Juvenile literature.
3. Archaeology—Juvenile literature. I. Title.
GN751.W65 2015
001.94—dc23

2014023244

Manufactured in the United States of America

Photo credits: Cover, p. 1 Cindi L/Shutterstock.com; pp. 4–5 © Fortean/TopFoto/The Image Works; pp. 7, 17, 25 De Agostini Picture Library/Getty Images; p. 9 swilmor/iStock/Thinkstock; p. 10 © Photos.com/Thinkstock; p. 12 © 1997; AISA, Archivo Iconográfico, Barcelona, España; p. 13 Culture Club/Hulton Archive/Getty Images; p. 15 C. Reyes/Shostal Associates; p. 19 The Bridgeman Art Library/Getty Images; p. 21 Hulton Archive/Getty Images; p. 22 Getty Research Institute/Photo Researchers, Inc.; p. 26 Print Collector/Hulton Archive/Getty Images; p. 29 Rachid Dahnoun/Getty Images; p. 31 De Agostini/Getty Images; p. 34 © Charles Walker/Topfoto/The Image Works; p. 35 © Jeffrey Alford/Asia Access; p. 37 © Beuna Vista/courtesy Everett Collection; p. 39 photo by ZUMA Archive/ZUMA Press © 2006 by ZUMA Archive; p. 41 Erica Brough/Gainsville Sun/Landov; interior pages background images © iStockphoto.com/Kivilvim Pinar, © iStockphoto.com/mitja2.

CONTENTS

INTRODUCTION

Legends of lost places or peoples have captured the imaginations of many different civilizations throughout history. Such tales have existed as long as humans have told each other stories.

One of the most famous and long-lived legends has been that of Atlantis. Atlantis first appeared in the classical Greek writings of the famous philosopher and mathematician Plato. Atlantis was said to be a once powerful island nation that was completely destroyed by a great disaster—one that submerged it beneath the ocean.

Many civilizations and cultures share such stories. Some of these tales were inspired by real places or events. Others were merely born from the vivid imaginations of storytellers. Lost cities of gold, ideal or magical places, and other mysterious sites have inspired exploration throughout the centuries. They have also been common subjects of literature and other media such as movies and television.

It is vital to investigate the origins of these stories, how they relate to reality, and also what makes them so popular with different cultures and peoples. By doing so, one can dive deep into the mysteries of Atlantis and other lost cities and begin to understand them.

The mythical lost civilization of Atlantis has inspired legends and speculation for centuries. It is often depicted as seen here: abandoned and submerged beneath the ocean, with architecture resembling that of ancient Greece or Rome.

CHAPTER ONE

PLATO'S ATLANTIS

O
ne of the first people to describe the legend of Atlantis in detail was Plato. Plato was one of the most important thinkers of ancient Greece. Around 360 BCE, Plato wrote *Timaeus*. This dialogue of Plato's mostly consists of a monologue—a kind of dramatic story or speech told by a sole speaker or narrator. Timaeus, the speaker, tells other characters, among them the famous philosopher Socrates, about the nature of the world and humanity.

Before Timaeus's monologue begins, however, another character named Critias first tells a tale about his fellow Athenian statesman, Solon. While traveling to Egypt, an Egyptian priest had told Solon of the battle between ancient Athens and another power. Beyond the Strait of Gibraltar, which connects the Mediterranean Sea with the Atlantic Ocean, there lay a large island,

Pictured here is a marble bust of Plato, the ancient Greek philosopher, writer, and mathematician whose mentions of Atlantis in his writings still intrigue readers and historians today.

"larger than Libya and Asia put together." This was the island of Atlantis.

Critias added that Atlantis "had rule over the whole island and several others, and over parts of the continent . . . The men of Atlantis had subjected the parts of Libya within the Pillars of Heracles [an ancient name for the Strait of Gibraltar] as far as Egypt, and of Europe as far as Tyrrhenia

PLATO, PHILOSOPHER AND THINKER

Plato's ideas and writings on philosophy, science, and math helped lay the foundations of Western civilization. Plato wrote many dialogues, stories in which characters explore moral or philosophical issues through conversation. It was a format invented by his teacher and mentor, Socrates. Along with Plato's student, Aristotle, the three are considered the greatest Western thinkers of their era.

Plato opened a school, the Academy at Athens, in about 387 BCE, to provide lessons in philosophy, law, and scientific research—primarily mathematics. Plato grew up during the decades of conflict with Sparta and other city-states. This conflict, coupled with the forced suicide of his teacher Socrates for political reasons in 399 BCE, is believed to have influenced some of his dialogues, including the ones involving Atlantis.

[a region of central Italy]." It was the leadership of Athens, the powerful city-state of ancient Greece, that defeated the Atlanteans when their kings tried to conquer more of the world.

The Rock of Gibraltar, located on the British territory also called Gibraltar, rises above the Strait of Gibraltar, which separates the Mediterranean Sea from the Atlantic Ocean to the west. It is beyond this strait where Atlantis was most famously rumored to be.

CRITIAS

Plato returns to Atlantis in much bolder detail in his next dialogue, *Critias*, named after the main narrator. Critias recounts that the Greek god of the sea, Poseidon, married a mortal woman. Their descendants came to rule over the

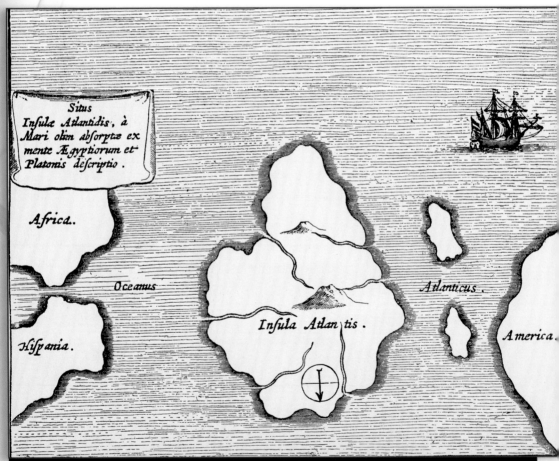

This 1664 engraving of Atlantis places the lost continent between Europe and Africa (left) and the Americas (right). The upper-left text translates to "The site of Atlantis, now beneath the sea, according to the beliefs of the Egyptians and the description of Plato."

island of Atlantis, whose unique geography was Poseidon's creation. Rings of land surrounded its center, and each ring was surrounded by a body of water. A canal ran through the center of this land to connect each ring to the sea. The island at the middle contained the capital of Atlantis, the city itself was said to be 11 miles (18 kilometers) wide.

Atlantis used its great national resources and riches to become one of the world's most powerful nations. The island of Atlantis had great forests, stone quarries used to construct its buildings, and fertile agricultural land. A mysterious metal known as orichalcum that was mentioned only in ancient writings was common on Atlantis. Ancient peoples considered orichalcum to be nearly as precious as gold. Unlike other places, Atlantis had a climate that allowed for two crop harvests a year, instead of the usual one. Many animals, especially elephants, roamed the island.

Over time, ten rulers came to split up the island. Each king ruled his section of Atlantis from a great city, and the ten kings lived together peacefully for a long time. No king was allowed to make war on another Atlantean king. The citizens led simple, virtuous lives. With time, however, they grew greedy and hungry for power, and their leaders sought to conquer other lands.

Atlantis threatened the civilizations of the Mediterranean, especially Athens and Egypt, about 9,000 years before Plato's account was written. Even though it outnumbered its enemies, Atlantis was defeated in an effort led primarily by the Athenians. Zeus and the other

The center of ancient Athens is known as the Acropolis. Despite outnumbering their enemies, the people of ancient Atlantis were said to have been defeated by an effort led by the Athenians.

gods were said to have grown angry at the pride and greed of the Atlanteans. Because of this, soon after its military defeat, the gods punished Atlantis with a massive earthquake and tidal waves that drowned the island nation within the span of just one night and day.

OTHER LOST CITIES: SODOM AND GOMORRAH

Much like Atlantis was said to have been a virtuous place that became slowly corrupted, the biblical tale of the cities of Sodom and Gomorrah also demonstrated lessons about right and wrong. These ancient cities were considered wicked, as illustrated in a section of the Bible in which Lot and his guests were treated poorly by the cities' residents. God supposedly destroyed the two cities with fire and brimstone as punishment for their wickedness.

In both the story of Atlantis and this biblical narrative, angry deities destroy a group of people for having defied their laws. The modern-day location of Sodom and Gomorrah is said to be along a southern peninsula of the Dead Sea, in Israel.

This engraving illustrates the famous biblical tale of Lot and his family escaping the destruction of Sodom and Gomorrah. Lot's wife—shown at left—was turned into a pillar of salt for disobediently looking back to see the burning cities.

PLATO'S LOST CONTINENT: REAL OR NOT?

Atlantis was likely just a fictional creation of Plato's. Rather than dealing with real people or places, many of his works were written to impart an idea of how ideal places or people should be. In this way, his works are lessons in how to behave or how to look at certain things.

One clue as to Plato's intentions was the date given for Atlantis's reign: the ninth millennium BCE. Even in Plato's time, most Greeks would not have believed that Athens already existed that far back in time. Plato's aim in writing about Atlantis may have been to help prevent the Greeks from making the same mistakes that the fictional Atlanteans had, so that they, too, would not be destroyed.

ATLANTIS AND THE NEW WORLD

During the Age of Discovery, Europeans were looking for new trade routes to reach Asia in the east, and new lands that they could conquer and claim as colonies. In Christopher Columbus's attempts to reach India by sailing to the west, he stumbled upon the Americas.

Initially driven by the Spanish and Portuguese, more and more European explorers arrived to carve out and conquer the lands of the peoples they discovered

The Temple of Inscriptions in Palenque, Mexico, is just one of the many architectural remains of the advanced Mayan civilization.

in the so-called New World. One of the most advanced civilizations of the ancient world, the Maya had existed in southern Mexico and Central America from the second millennium BCE.

The Maya were recognized for their advanced art, architecture, government, written language, and exploration of the sciences. Many Europeans throughout the centuries had assumed that their own civilization was superior to that of all peoples of the New World. These Europeans sought an explanation for why the Maya were, in their opinion, so much more advanced than other New World peoples.

MAYANISM

Charles Étienne Brasseur de Bourbourg, a 19th-century French writer, traveled to the Americas to study Mayan ruins on behalf of the Catholic Church. While his travels contributed greatly to European knowledge, they also gave rise to interesting but inaccurate theories about the Maya—a set of ideas and beliefs called Mayanism.

Mayanism theorized that the Maya were somehow connected to the histories of the Ten Lost Tribes of Israel, the original Tower of Babel, or even Noah and the Flood. Each of these three biblical narratives relates how the ancient peoples described in the Hebrew Bible (also known as the Old Testament) were dispersed, travelling and forming new civilizations. Those Europeans who believed that

Atlantis had been a real place were convinced that the Maya were somehow connected to the lost continent.

These theories, which were rooted in speculation, can be considered pseudoscience, and have proven to

Another tale of destruction in the Hebrew Bible was the story of Noah and the Great Flood, depicted here in a detail from a thirteenth-century mosaic in the Basilica of St. Marco, in Venice, Italy. Some Mayanists attempted to link the story of the Great Flood with the destruction of Atlantis.

be entirely false. Some of them were rooted in hateful or racist beliefs, such as the superiority of Europeans. Explorers believed that the native peoples they found in the New World could not have created the advanced civilizations they discovered. Instead, they insisted that a mysterious third group must have been responsible for the Mayan innovations.

OTHER LOST CITIES: CÍBOLA'S SEVEN CITIES OF GOLD

Another legend inspired by the Spaniards' desire for riches in the New World was that of the Seven Golden Cities of Cíbola. The fabulous cities were first reported by Álvar Núñez Cabeza de Vaca who, after being shipwrecked off Florida in 1528, had wandered through what later became Texas and northern Mexico before his rescue in 1536. The viceroy of New Spain, Antonio de Mendoza, sent an expedition in 1539 to verify Cabeza de Vaca's reports. Fray Marcos de Niza, a Franciscan friar sent on that expedition, claimed to have seen them in the distance.

In 1540, the conquistador Francisco Vásquez de Coronado was sent to search for cities where houses were made of gold and streets were paved with it. Coronado's men never found Cíbola. Instead, they clashed with the native peoples they encountered, including Zuni Indians in New Mexico. They made it as far as present-day Kansas, but found no golden cities.

THE SEARCH FOR EL DORADO

Among the resources European explorers sought in the Americas, gold and other precious metals were top priorities. The Spanish discovered great riches while conquering

This painting illustrates the legend of El Dorado, or "the Golden Man," being held aloft by his servants. The city of El Dorado was a legend among the Spanish during their conquest of the Americas. Today, numerous towns and sites throughout South America are said to be the location of the legend.

the Aztec and Inca Empires, and greed drove them to seek even more. These riches, coupled with the advanced Mayan society the Europeans had encountered, led to popular myths and lore about what else the newly discovered continent kept hidden. Tales and rumors grew about other, even richer rulers and cities hidden in the jungles and mountains of the Americas.

One ruler, said to plaster his body with gold dust during rituals and then wash himself off in Lake Guatavita (located in modern Colombia), was called El Dorado, or "the Gilded One." Soon, El Dorado came to mean entire cities of gold, and even a whole mythical nation of gold. Conquistadors and other Spaniards and Portuguese searched all over to find these cities. While no such gilded city was ever actually found, the search for one did speed up the European colonization of South, Central, and North America.

MYTHS OF THE NEW WORLD: THE FOUNTAIN OF YOUTH

One of the most famous legendary lost sites in the New World was a spring called the Fountain of Youth. Juan Ponce de León, the first European known to visit the mainland United States, became famous for his search for this magical site, which was alleged to be a spring or fountain that kept those who drank from it perpetually young.

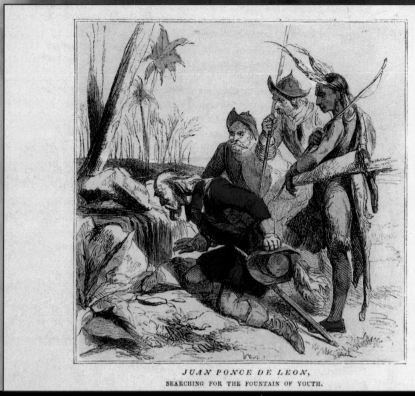

JUAN PONCE DE LEON,
SEARCHING FOR THE FOUNTAIN OF YOUTH.

In this print from 1754, Spanish explorer Juan Ponce de León is shown during his quest for the island of Bimini, the reputed location of the legendary Fountain of Youth. He is shown accompanied by fellow Spaniards and an indigenous American guide.

Initially, the fountain was believed to exist on the Bahamian island of Bimini. Ponce de León led a mission from Puerto Rico in March 1513, but the Fountain of Youth remained elusive. But, he was the first European to enter the ocean current known as the Gulf Stream and to sight Florida. He landed near the current site of the city of St. Augustine, the oldest still existing European settlement in North America. To this day an archaeological park in St. Augustine hosts the spring purported to be the one about which Ponce de León wrote.

SEARCHING FOR ATLANTIS IN AMERICA

Inspired by those explorers who came before them, some investigators have looked for evidence of Atlantean

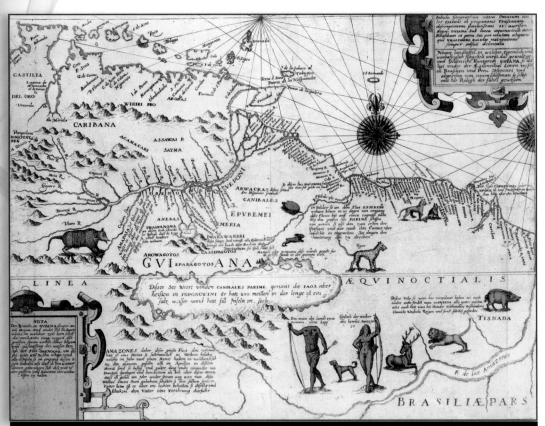

The search for El Dorado in the areas around modern Guyana, Venezuela, and Brazil gave rise to new legends among the Spanish and other Europeans that included stories of headless men called the Ewaipanoma. The British explorer Sir Walter Raleigh first wrote about them during his seventeenth-century travels.

influence in the ruins of pre-Columbian civilizations throughout Central and South America.

In 1998 anthropologist George Erikson and his partner Ivar Zapp published a book in which they theorized that Atlantis may have existed in the Caribbean or Yucatan regions of Central and South America. They claim that the catastrophic event that destroyed it was a huge volcanic eruption, an earthquake, or a large asteroid or comet that hit either the Bahamas, the Yucatan Peninsula, or another nearby region. Survivors of this disaster, say Erikson and Zapp, most likely helped start the various advanced civilizations of the Americas.

Even among those who believe that Atlantis was a real, historical place, most say that it was unlikely that Atlantis existed in the Americas. It would have been too far and difficult a journey for any such news of a place like Atlantis to reach the Greeks or the Egyptians. They also point out that many of the stories of this lost civilization seem to imply that it possessed technology far greater than any that existed in other ancient civilizations. Thus, they logically conclude that these are mere stories, and not serious theories.

CHAPTER THREE

THE REAL ATLANTIS

Was there ever a real place called Atlantis, a civilization that was wiped out and drowned beneath the oceans? Could the tale be the fictional version of a real historical event? Many historians, archaeologists, and pseudoscientists argue about these questions. Efforts to figure out whether Atlantis was real include serious historical inquiry, as well as some more unconventional, paranormal investigations.

THE ERUPTION AT THERA

There is no real proof from scientists or historians that huge earthquakes or floods happened around the time when Atlantis was alleged to have drowned, but comparable events at other times might have inspired the story.

This ancient fresco, dated 1650 BCE, shows a flotilla, or group, of Minoan ships. The island civilization of Minoa relied heavily on its navy and suffered greatly from a natural disaster that many believe influenced Plato's account of Atlantis's destruction.

One very real ancient disaster was the volcanic eruption of Thera. This event was also known as the Minoan eruption because of the Minoan civilization that existed on the island of Crete dating back to around 3000 BCE. The volcano Thera, on the island of the same name, erupted sometime around the year 1500 BCE.

Scientists speculate that the Theran eruption was comparable to some of the most powerful explosive events of all time, including other famous eruptions, such as the volcanic eruption of Mt. Vesuvius that destroyed ancient Pompeii in 79 CE, and the more recent eruption of Mount St. Helens in Washington State in 1980. Historical accounts seem to vary, but it is likely that thousands died from the eruption at Thera and its aftermath.

Even worse, tsunamis (or tidal waves) caused by the eruption did great damage to the Minoans' fleets and ports. The amount of ash released was so great that it dropped temperatures in the region by a few degrees. Weather itself was disrupted, and regional harvests failed. Later, the Minoans were invaded and conquered by their neighbors.

Shown here is an 1866 eruption on the island of Santorini (formerly known as Thera). The island has experienced several volcanic events throughout history, and its modern horseshoe shape is even a consequence of the famed eruption that occurred around 1500 BCE.

The story of Atlantis's fall and the actual events that ruined the Minoan civilization are very similar. It is possible that the ancient Greeks knew that Plato was drawing upon this historical event in his fictional account. Another theory is that retellings of the eruption from sources in nearby Egypt may also have influenced Plato.

The Atlantis legend might also have had ties to stories later passed down in the Hebrew Bible, including the stories of Noah and the Flood. The biblical plagues of Egypt may also have had similar historical roots.

OTHER LOST CITIES: CAMELOT

From the Middle Ages in Britain, stories arose of a virtuous and just king and his court, King Arthur Pendragon, and their battles against evil and injustice. Arthur's court was seated in the castle called Camelot. It included the Knights of the Round Table, spawning

Gustave Doré's 1868 engraving shows Camelot, home of the Arthurian knights.

many stories over the centuries, known as the "Arthurian legends."

The term *Camelot* has come to be associated with the values and morals displayed by Arthur and his court, the symbol of chivalry and justice. It also refers to a peaceful time and idealistic period led by a strong leader. Later, in the United States, the presidency of John F. Kennedy was often referred to as Camelot. Scholars and others have claimed various places to be the "real" Camelot, including castles in Wales and England.

LOST, NOT FOUND

Professionals of all kinds—including archaeologists, researchers, historians, and anthropologists—have suggested many different regions of the world as the possible site of Atlantis.

One popular theory has been that Spartel Bank is a remnant of Atlantis. This submerged island lies off the coast of Spain, and it is about 184 feet (56 meters) beneath the water's surface. Spartel Bank has intrigued those seeking Atlantis because it is estimated to have been historically above sea level until a tsunami submerged it between 11,500 and 12,000 years ago. This timeline matches Plato's account. However, the only remains of this island consist of a mud shoal, and even when it was still on the surface, the island was much smaller than any accounts of Atlantis.

Others have suggested theories that Atlantis existed in other places, including somewhere near the

This famous lighthouse stands at Cape Spartel, at the northwestern tip of Morocco, marking the Atlantic entrance to the Strait of Gibraltar. It lies near Spartel Bank, one of the rumored possible sites of Atlantis.

Canary Islands, west of the coast of Africa; near Finland or Sweden; or on any of the major Mediterranean islands, including Sardinia, Sicily, Cyprus, Malta, or Thera (now Santorini). In fact, the explanation that the Theran eruption directly influenced the legend of Atlantis is perhaps the most sound. Other proposed scenarios even include the idea that the ruins of Atlantis exist beneath the ice sheets at the North Pole or Antarctica. No definitive evidence has substantially backed any of these proposed locations in a meaningful way.

29

ATLANTEAN ALIENS, REINCARNATION, AND PAST LIVES

From the 19th century through the 20th century and even up until today, many people who believe in paranormal phenomena such as past lives, reincarnation, alien life forms, and more have connected their belief systems to the legend of Atlantis. Some believe that the advanced technologies described in some legends of the island could only have come from outer-space visitors settling on Earth many thousands of years ago.

In addition, self-professed mystic and psychic Edgar Cayce (1877–1945), who greatly influenced the New Age movement, claimed that many of the people he interviewed while in a trance could describe in detail their past lives as citizens of Atlantis.

Some have even put forth theories that suggest that the site of ancient Atlantis corresponds to the mysterious Bermuda Triangle, a section of the Atlantic Ocean east of Florida where many ships and airplanes have supposedly disappeared over the last century.

A SPANISH EXPEDITION

In 2011 a U.S.-led research team claimed to have found evidence of Atlantis's existence in a marshland near

The historic Spanish port city of Cádiz, in the Andalusia region of Spain, is shown here in an aerial view. Its immediate surroundings have also been proffered as a possible former site of Atlantis.

the city of Cádiz in Spain. Because Cádiz rests on the Atlantic coast just outside the Strait of Gibraltar, many believed this site matched Plato's description of Atlantis's location. German physicist Rainer Kühne told *National Geographic* magazine in 2004 that satellite photos showed "rectangular structures and concentric circles that match very well with Plato's description of the palaces and the city of Atlantis."

Others, such as Swedish geographer Ulf Erlingsson, counter that another island is perhaps an even more obvious choice for the site of the former Atlantis: Ireland. Erlingsson points out that the island's size—300 miles (480 kilometers) long and 200 miles (320 kilometers) wide—and geographic features make it a close match to Plato's original description of Atlantis. Still other researchers remain skeptical about any such claims. So far, no one has provided concrete proof that such a civilization ever existed in any of these places.

CHAPTER FOUR

BROUGHT TO LIFE: ATLANTIS AND OTHER LOST CITIES IN POPULAR CULTURE

E ver since modern mass media has existed, fantastic tales of places like Atlantis have been a popular subject for writers, filmmakers, and other artists. They have also provided many localities around the world with tourist attractions that draw curious visitors.

ATLANTIS: THE ANTEDILUVIAN WORLD

During the 19th century, books became a popular form of entertainment for growing numbers of people. Ignatius Donnelly (1831–1901), a U.S. congressman for Minnesota, was a popular science writer of the time. Donnelly thought Plato's descriptions of Atlantean

This map of Atlantis, once again placing the lost continent in the mid-Atlantic Ocean, was an inspiration for Ignatius Donnelly's work.

civilization were mainly true. Brasseur de Bourbourg's research also influenced him greatly. Donnelly thought that all great ancient civilizations descended from Atlantis, including the ancient Maya.

He published his ideas in 1882 as *Atlantis: The Antediluvian World*. The word "antediluvian" means "before the deluge" [or flood]. This deluge refers to the history of humans before the story of Noah and the Ark from the Hebrew Bible. According to Donnelly, the Atlantean civilization had existed in that period. It also had been the first to bring humans from a primitive state to an advanced one.

Donnelly thought all of humanity's myths and legends that envisioned a paradise or perfect place were rooted in the memory of Atlantis. The Atlanteans supposedly emigrated from Atlantis and then populated the shores of the Gulf of Mexico, the Pacific coast of the Americas, the Mediterranean, and many other regions. People as far apart as the ancient Egyptians and the Incan people of Peru were originally Atlanteans, according to Donnelly. He claimed that ancient Egypt had a culture and civilization closest to that of the original Atlanteans.

OTHER LOST CITIES: SHANGRI-LA

In 1933 James Hilton's novel *Lost Horizon* became an influential best seller. In it, the main characters escape a rebellion in India when their plane is hijacked to Tibet. They end up in the mystical valley of Shangri-La, which is protected and hidden from the outside world.

Shangri-La is a place of harmony. Its inhabitants live in peace and happiness, and their lives are

The Tarim Basin region of northwest China, near Tibet, is a rumored site for the mythical Shangri-La.

extremely long, so long, in fact, that the people are almost immortal. Like Atlantis and other lost cities, Shangri-La was portrayed as an ideal place, where knowledge and virtue were treasured. There, the escaped characters find the inner peace they were looking for in a war-torn world. The term *Shangri-La* became a synonym for any paradise hidden from mankind. Sometimes, it stands in for any form of perfection that people look for in the world.

LOST CITIES ONSCREEN

Tales of fantasy were among the first stories to which motion picture audiences flocked. For that reason, Atlantis and places based on it were portrayed onscreen from the earliest days of cinema. Among the first films was *Undersea Kingdom*, made in 1936. The heroes of this movie, Lieutenant Crash Corrigan and Professor Norton, lead an expedition to find Atlantis because one of the leaders of the Atlanteans, an evil dictator, is threatening to destroy mankind. Another epic Hollywood production, *Atlantis: The Lost Continent* (1961), painted a more classic portrayal, depicting the destruction of the island nation in ancient times.

Later movie versions of Atlantis became extremely popular with recent generations of children. Disney's beloved 1989 cartoon film, *The Little Mermaid*, is partially set in the undersea realm of Atlantica, which is influ-

Atlantis: The Lost Empire *was a 2001 Disney animated feature starring voice actors such as Michael J. Fox and Leonard Nimoy. It tells the tale of a young man who finds a little-known text that leads him and his companions to the lost city of Atlantis.*

enced by Atlantis (although its inhabitants include both humans and talking sea creatures). In 2001 Disney produced *Atlantis: The Lost Empire*, an animated adventure in which a young man discovers evidence of the lost city 10,000 years after it disappeared under the ocean.

Lost cities of the New World have also been featured in films and other media throughout the years. Werner Herzog's acclaimed 1972 adventure, *Aguirre, the Wrath of God*, features a partially fictionalized Spanish conquistador searching for El Dorado in South America. DreamWorks Studios produced an animated adventure comedy in 2000 called *The Road to El Dorado*. In it, two men cheat at a game of dice in 16th-century Spain and win a map of the rumored city of gold. They hitch a ride with Hernán Cortés's expedition to the New World. When they find the famed city, its inhabitants mistake them for gods.

Shangri-La, too, has been the focus of popular films. Hilton's 1933 novel *Lost Horizon* was turned into a movie with the same name by director Frank Capra in 1937.

ATLANTIS IN OTHER MEDIA

Some modern narratives envision Atlantis as a place that still secretly exists under the sea. Throughout the 20th century, comic books have been a popular form of entertainment. The Marvel Comics universe—home to characters such as the Avengers, the X-Men, and Spider-Man—even has its own version of Atlantis. Marvel Comic's Sub-Mariner tells of the adventures of Prince Namor, the half-human leader of Atlantis. Prince Namor's father is a human sea captain, and his mother belongs to the *Homo mermanus* race of under-sea-dwelling, water-breathing Atlanteans.

This postage stamp depicts Aquaman, a DC Comics superhero who rules over Atlantis.

DC Comics, the source of beloved heroes such as Superman and Batman, have their own Atlantean hero: Aquaman. Aquaman is the defender of the underwater kingdom of Atlantis and a member of the superhero consortium, the Justice League of America. He debuted

VISITORS WELCOME!

Many places around the world embrace these legends of lost cities, such as Atlantis, El Dorado, and others. Oftentimes they are a point of pride for locals in the sites where they are alleged to have existed, and they also help those places attract visiting tourists who support their local economies.

St. Augustine, Florida, for example, has turned the original site of Ponce de León's settlement into the Fountain of Youth Archaeological Park. The Bimini Road, an underwater rock formation in the Bahamas, has also attracted many tourists, divers, and researchers wanting to judge if it is man-made and perhaps a relic of Atlantis. Thousands of tourists also flock to Thera (now called Santorini) and drink the locally made "Atlantis" wine.

in 1941 and is a popular character to this day.

Atlantis has also frequently surfaced in video and role-playing games for decades. Even where it is not named explicitly, many such games—whether they are games of strategy or first-person shooter games—contain undersea kingdoms or cities as settings that are directly influenced by the story of Atlantis.

CONCLUSION

Ultimately, whether or not we find definitive evidence of the existence of cities such as Atlantis, to call these fabled societies "lost cities" is inaccurate. Legendary

A park employee holds a cup of spring water from the Spring House at the Fountain of Youth Archaeological Park in St. Augustine, Florida. Lost cities and similar legends provide many communities worldwide with tourist revenue.

lands such as Cíbola, El Dorado, and Camelot—while most likely entirely imaginary—persist in popular imagination across the world. For researchers, they provide the motivation to continue exploring and seeking the truth. For science fiction fans or enthusiasts of the paranormal, the legends will continue to inspire debate, and more importantly, stir the imagination.

GLOSSARY

AGE OF DISCOVERY A period of European exploration of the world between the 15th and 18th centuries.

ANTEDILUVIAN Relating to the period before the flood described in the Hebrew Bible.

CONCENTRIC Refers to objects that share the same center or axis; for example, the circles in a bull's-eye target.

CONQUISTADOR Spanish for "conqueror." Conquistadores were military men from Spain who explored and conquered the New World.

DIALOGUE A dramatic entertainment or written work in which two or more characters exchange spoken or written conversation.

GILDED Covered in gold leaf or gold paint.

MAYANISM A set of inaccurate beliefs about the Maya people of Mexico and Central America that claims they are descendants of ancient peoples of the Old World.

MONOLOGUE A long uninterrupted speech delivered by one person in the presence of others.

NEW AGE Refers to a set of alternative belief systems and approaches to medicine and faith that differ from traditional Western ones.

NEW WORLD The continents of North and South America, so-called because they were new to European explorers centuries ago.

ORICHALCUM A fictional metal mentioned in Greek writings that is nearly as valuable as gold.

PERPETUALLY Continuing forever or everlasting.

PILLARS OF HERACLES The ancient name for the Strait of Gibraltar.

PSEUDOSCIENCE A set of beliefs that are mistakenly believed to be based on scientific fact.

REIGN A period during which a leader or a nation rules over a group of people.

REINCARNATION The rebirth of the soul in a new body; in some faiths or belief systems, such as Hinduism, this occurs again and again.

QUARRIES Large, deep pits from which people remove stone and other building materials.

REALM A kingdom, country, or land.

TSUNAMI A large ocean wave caused by an earthquake or other disturbance.

VIRTUOUS Exhibiting high moral standards.

FOR FURTHER READING

Abrams, Dennis. *Atlantis* (Lost Worlds and Mysterious Civilizations). New York: Chelsea House, 2012.

Crompton, Samuel Willard. *Troy* (Lost Worlds and Mysterious Civilizations). New York, NY: Chelsea House, 2012.

Ganeri, Anita. *Lost in the Bermuda Triangle and Other Mysteries* (Incredible True Adventures). New York, NY: Rosen Publishing, 2012.

Hawkins, John. *Atlantis and Other Lost Worlds.* New York, NY: Rosen Publishing, 2012.

Lee, Tony, and Sam Hart. *Excalibur: The Legend of King Arthur* (Heroes & Heroines). Somerville, MA: Candlewick Press, 2011.

Mountjoy, Shane. *The Maya* (Lost Worlds and Mysterious Civilizations). New York, NY: Chelsea House, 2012.

Plato. *Timaeus and Critias.* Edited by Thomas Kjeller Johansen. Translated by Desmond Lee. New York, NY: Penguin, 2008.

Pye, Michael, and Kirsten Dalley. *Lost Cities and For-gotten Civilizations*. New York, NY: Rosen Publishing, 2013.

Rinaldo, Denise. *Cities of the Dead: Finding Lost Civilizations* (24/7: Science Behind the Scenes: Mystery Files). New York, NY: Children's Press, 2008.

Wagner, Heather Lehr. *Pompeii* (Lost Worlds and Mysterious Civilizations). New York, NY: Chelsea House, 2012.

WEBSITES

Because of the changing nature of Internet links, Rosen Publishing has developed an online list of websites related to the subject of this book. This site is updated regularly. Please use this link to access the list:

http://www.rosenlinks.com/UTP/Atlan

INDEX